Then and Now

by Ellen Bari

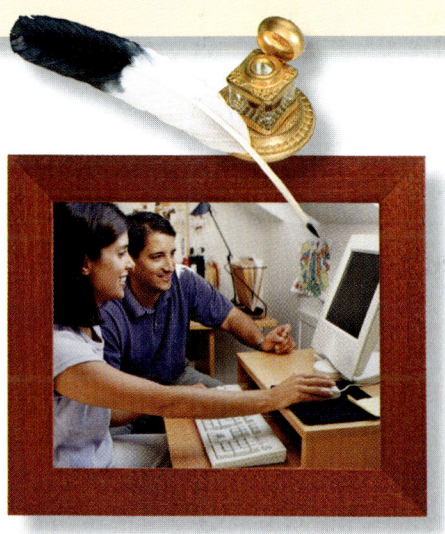

PEARSON

Scott Foresman

Editorial Offices: Glenview, Illinois • Parsippany, New Jersey • New York, New York
Sales Offices: Needham, Massachusetts • Duluth, Georgia • Glenview, Illinois
Coppell, Texas • Ontario, California • Mesa, Arizona

Long Ago

Long ago, many people in the United States built houses made of wood. A **neighborhood** is a **community** of many houses built close together.

Today

Today, we still build houses made out of wood. We also use glass, brick, or steel to build houses. Many houses in the United States have running water and **electricity**.

Long Ago

Long ago, many people wrote letters by hand. They used a pen and paper. They sent these letters to family and friends.

Today

Today, many people also send e-mails from computers. The e-mails arrive fast!

Long Ago

Long ago, many people traveled on horseback. It took a long time to get places.

Today

Today, cars and buses travel on roads. Many highways make travel fast and easy.

Glossary

community a group of people and the place where they live

electricity a form of energy

neighborhood a place where people live, work, and play